PRETTY YOUNG THING
DANIELLE PAFUNDA

D1226094

PRETTY YOUNG THING
DANIELLE PAFUNDA

Soft Skull Press / Brooklyn, NY

Soft Skull Press
www.softskull.com
Distributed by Publishers Group West
www.pgw.com | 800.788.3123

Library of Congress Cataloging-in-Publication Data
Pafunda, Danielle.
    Pretty young thing : poems / Danielle Pafunda.
        p. cm.
    ISBN-13: 978-1-932360-97-4 (alk. paper)
    ISBN-10: 1-932360-97-2 (alk. paper)
    I. Title.

PS3616.A3366P74 2005
811'.6--dc22

2005019656

I.

Maybe I really will become a fish. Then you won't be able to see me. At the lakeside early in the morning you will see only a fine, tiny fish jump from the water and move its lips to you and disappear. Then your heart will be torn to pieces and your head will spin like a windmill.

—CAN XUE

I saved part of the infection in a small plastic bag. A grievance.
You didn't want me. To turn down your covers, or generate
a low tone. You were wet with radiation sickness.
A pair of eyes came out of you. A pair of wisdom teeth,
a practice...

Eventually, I pinned your left hand behind your back. I sang you,
that boat, that heaven, the three-armed love. Whether there was
a blind wind on. When the sash blew we knew it was close.
The hoodlum tundra, the icicle full of pills. When the first
and perfect, and each one its own tome...

Even my breakage. In the closet, I shook the vehicle. In the
back of the closet, I examined my own fur.

Took my hand off the handlebars. Took my hand off the suitcase.
Took my hands out of my pockets and they were the white pages
of a new diary. A stolen diary, and ready to chuck in the snow.

Other times I might've told you a little something about yourself.
How you went to the circus and the lion pissed on your mother.
How you ate Japanese pancakes, or had your chest x-rayed for arrowheads.
But this was all before New Year's. You were standing ankle-deep
on the roof on the other side of town. The fireworks were loused up.

On a lone walk around the park. Counterclockwise or poorly executed.

Every night I positioned my pillow to catch the bullet. I kept my teeth
in an intimate place and never heard the machines in the basement. I heard
choir on the street, and was glad for you. I was glad for your girlfriend,
your parents, brother, mascot, tigress, clipper and a few lights
coming in off the bridge. Maybe the boats.

By accident, I called the president *Daddy*. Wasted, one glazier
after another took off his big shoes and put them up on the table.
The press conference shook the television as the bartenderess
came through with a tray of shot, all cast as a vote.

I was hoping they'd be interchangeable. Hoping I was old enough
to go without my girlfriends. A string of birds is like one of pearls
when the hunter gets back. Wherein pearls are like worms, and
the stories about pogrom end in a bird's wing. Wherein the gingerbread,
rife with buckshot, worn with larvae.

When I got out in the weather, the weather was missing. The hour
slit like an electric cord, splintered, and fused to the pavement.
There was a space in the road where I thought a handsome cab should be.
There was really a space, and you would've been here to fill it.

Be pretty with me now; I'm not ready for anything else.
The pet is at the door, making her little noises that ask.
I don't have a lot of time; don't take it personally.

There's a headache hanging near the ceiling, waiting
to *take root,* like they say of dandelion seed, of a fetus.
Like they say in retrospect about the catchy despot,

or the dirty palliatives on the table.

So, okay, let's take off clothes. Go on and measure me,
but don't look at me too long. The magazines set a limit.
Scientific. Five minutes. Let's get going, get it on

and over so you can get me a drink. I'm in it for my own
reasons. I'm in my cups, in glass slippers, there's a glass
in your hand. By the bed.

Wrote the name of the pill on my hand. Wrote *one*
because that was all I took. I spent a long time making the bed.
It wasn't because you weren't home, so much as it wasn't home
without you there. I didn't want to make any mistakes.
Took the trash out early, and washed the bottles in the sink.
I wasn't sad. I was occupied.

The cat was in heat and every advisement involved a Bic pen.
The television broke, the toaster inflamed. Around three there was nothing
in the air but air, and I wasn't asleep. Wrote the name of the pill, wrote
my name, wrote yours. Wrote a couple things I'd been meaning to do.
Wrote *married* and wondered.

Even in good dreams, I take a piss in the wrong place. I wake up
with sweat between my legs, my hands numb, and thinking
you're down there at the end of the bed setting up nets
and all kinds of measures.

Fable

When he was mine, I'd milk him. Make his hair
grow. He was, at first, a liar. He was actually
employed by the circus. He was a fandango.
A woman with a nine-foot penis. An inch.

The ghosts of two wives met him at the foot
of the bed. The first with resin-coated hairpiece
and second with red nail lacquer. No. He was
only afraid of the little wolves who lived behind
the little wool skirts. Of girls in closets.

I pooled his underwear around my own ankles.
The cordite hairs on his back sang a chorus. I took.
His pockets, complicit. I gave, too. A plump.
My lithesome peacock, fanned tail feathers. The cinder.

On Cinco de Mayo, you get shot in the head with a pellet gun.
The doctor, my finger makes rounds on your temple. The boys
swing their two-by-four. The amorphous piñata.

A mouthful of Corona and trolling for cops, I'm an unlikely
fish on the street. Unlikely in my broken boots and cheap jacket.
A bodega dog is on a loop and the bartenders back away.

Condoms, candy, tiny kaleidoscopes, and my blindfold gets lost
in the park. Fireworks leak onto the sidewalk. Twits leak out
of a rolling taxi. The night watchmen are cranky. I take ten dollars
out of my purse.

The boys start to yelling. The park to leaning in the wind, the bar
to spinning, and someone tall jumps at the fire escape. My knee
turns at the curb where a garbage can stops me. Anyway, it's time.
I got you some ice, but it melted. I got a couple of phone numbers
and a free sample cologne.

A FASHION

With two types of beer mingling in the plastic cups. Dirty.
Like kink, like two at a time. We were made to be polite.
At the beer garden, under the ospreys, with good teeth.

Faster pussycat kill kill. The hips gone at it down in the gravel.
A handful. Also wanted the roadster. Wanted to be off-road
with racing stripes, anywhere other than Brooklyn or Queens.
Wanted to chase you down on the sand with a pint of something
sweet brown between us.

To tug you around by the collar of your white T-shirt. Pin you against
the wall in the bathroom, familiar, littoral. To hold red lipstick very,
very close to your cheek and say, *I'm sorry.* Wanted both of us
to have bigger tits and an easier time of it. To be drunk enough to believe
a beach and come out in swimsuits, with hula hoops, flashing our hands.

So drunk it felt like Christmas, I rolled my tongue over each one
of your abacus beads. Tarantula, tarantella conflated for good reason.
The kitchen was, regrettably, in 6/8 time.

Increased police presence was only making it worse. Still unused
to the megaphoned voices reordering the street, still unused
to the monomania of blue disco. Rather, pull the blinds.
Exacerbated a portion of liquor with a portion of raw onion. A mistake
in the sequence of alt, slick, luck.

And the boatman was not friendly.

COURTESY

I took a bite from the wormy part for the cur in my stomach.
My plastic, my porcelain stomach. My lover, he wore a buzzer
in the palm of his heart. A hot rod. My lover was a dry heave.
I pinned my hair for him, with a bat bone. I pinned the page
to the wall of the discount drugstore. An advertisement for tricks.

They put the broads on a broad street and the clinicians above
the drugstore. The deference to the white coat and round eye
of the stethoscope. The chill in my lover's fingers was a false
negative. A falsie. I took a pint for the first five days and
a pint–point–five for the rest.

I slit my skirt. I slit the turf around my garden bed. I lay it
with torn news and vegetable scraps. I lit my tongue in the slit
of an envelope. A reverse. A recipe inside. My lover wore
chef's gloves, for fighting the eager meat. For the quick
he cut me.

NET

At the opening, I couldn't think of a thing pornographic. The gallery
was a box and the curator's hair had germinated. In her office,
the underside of her desk was wired. Sure, her stockings were shorn.
The artists themselves, with a pair of Exacto blades. Sure, the program
confirmed the location of each of their mothers.

The thing about Time Square, said they, is the closer you get, the more
the electricity costs. You don't need a weatherman, you need a barometer.
You should have been told so in health class. Convinced, I took a cab.
I took my vibrator in my purse, just in case. It pays to count the change.

The truth was, I didn't drink, which they didn't believe. Especially when I did,
but really it was social and I never inhaled. I couldn't inhale. I had two
kinds of pants: small and smaller. For these events. Hors d'oeuvres
contaminated the perimeter. Loose digits. We were flat broke, after all,
and even my credit cards grew wings and expired.

With rusted, borrowed fin. With pink plastic seaweed.
With a ring pop ring. The junkyard mermaid of wedding gowns
and the smell of the aquarium sold them on it. The food
by the shark tanks and the gifts with the anemones. Or else
it was beachy-keen. With the groom's pant legs rolled, Long Island
on the turntable, and the chicken dance on the grill.

There was a multiplicity of mothers of the bride. There was
a final auction on the bouquet. Anywhere you hang your hat
is home is heart is. Blew out to sea. He took her forearm
like a kite and went running. A sailboat. Or else the Italians
had them over a barrel. A fine Tuscan wine.

A year full of horses. Out of the corner of her eye. And the maids
were men and the ushers were well. Her veil puffed.

I RSVP'd as the wraith in the toga. The creeps, they had a good laugh.
I put on my jokes with a cheap blush. The vestments, a day old,
a dollar short. The bread was two days old. I felt like Lily Bart,
but not so sudden. Besides, the white gown was a plaintiff.
Besides, the drugstore was officious.

Where was the nicest mixer on the block and a good set of knives?
I needed a chemical peel. I needed a box of pantiliner, an enema.
Where was New Orleans in relation to that stake in the vegetable
garden? I had an empty day planner. An empty day planned.
I had full authority over the vehicle, a license, a blind spot.

On an empty stomach, the train floor looks like *happy*,
like a little yellow sweater. I could get up and keep going
car to car until I stepped out the back door, climbed the railing.

The destination doesn't really approach. The landscape is any.
A paper bag greases my feet; doesn't know Dallas from Detroit.
And *nothing goes with this dress*. Nothing goes.

The train grows cramped when I work it up that I've left
something behind. It's like that old joke—*What Gilda Ate*.
Keeps its forward motion, its track affinity.

Medicinal, perfunctory, uncooperative; but don't stop.

MISCONCEPTION

Felt like a good secret. The first secret I wanted to keep
to myself. If it was a rock in my pocket, it was a better rock.
A red rock, a named rock, a child's fist and a planet
for a child to assemble.

Felt like my piece, my line in the play about gods.
My name on a headstone for the living. If it was
just part of the story, it was the round part, warmed
with a brick, held in a blanket between two large thighs.

It didn't last long.

The next day I took my tongue to the mirror. I thought
about everything I'd ever licked: a banister, an ice cube,
a cotton nightgown, a streak of shit and a dog bone. Everything
I said bore a trace of talcum powder. It was possible
I'd actually used.

II.

The dead little girl says, I am the one who guffaws in horror inside the lungs of the live one. Get me out of there at once.

—ANTONIN ARTAUD

NOMENCLATURE

If they've been trying to kill me, it's the threat
that's dead. Where is that loving feeling?
Is my weakness for American flags? Is the
tack on the tongue? Is the beer ever sweet?
Wanted to call him *daddy, pop, poppa,* or *pappy.*
Her; she was a bat, a shit. *Lovey.*

Two girls on a trapeze came up in the lyrics.
They always wondered what two girls could do.

Rich, Lovey drove a sports car. A Camaro Z28.
A canary in the sack. She did rock stars. She did sing.

What floatation device did I take to get here?
A deal that I cut. Cut out with a sequined panty,
the house keys, the car keys, an emergency quarter
in my boot, an emergency. Someone boil the water.
Someone cut the bed sheets to rags. Someone find
the baby. She's out of the stomach. She's a stomach
of her own. A surname.

My head swelled up in 1980. My swelling swelled, my arms
and legs were not so sweet. I took my pants off in a green room.
My shirt. I took a seat on the ugly rocking horse. They called it
an x-ray. To lick me.

I used my doll as a shield. The place was a *child's*. It was my birthday.
My pants, my shirt, my undershirt. A needle came with its own empty
brain. They told me to make a fist. They told me to.

I got my own room with a clown in a bubble. When midnight
was punctured, I licked the pill from its middle. All the books
bore a yellowing. All the toys. I was content with a red crayon.

Everyone pointed out how good the bald boy was.

After a dozen vials none of us were any closer. More applesauce.

Midnight became regular.

The pill, sour and breathless.

It wasn't Texas, it just felt that way. Only dangerous
if you didn't like men. And I liked them.
The same way I liked the big belt my dad wore
through airport security, with its buckle, with its gun in the buckle.
The bullets were round, and snapped into place.

Buffalo meat tasted like a bite on the tongue,
a touch saltier than anyone else's. My long legs
even longer back then. There was no room
in the laps of those relatives for a small girl
seeing as the small girl was long gone. Instead
I stood around laughing, thinking vinegar things.

Black widows on my uncle's back porch with the safety off.
They nested near the weird plastic arm
that crushed twelve cases of cans that weekend.
Dried beetles were dinner and decoration,
their webs went forever if I squinted.
Nobody said anything. I made my normal face.

If I wasn't cleaning a plate, I was cleaning a plate,
straddling the line because I was ten. It was okay

to look at the guns, the video tape, the knitting
in my aunt's bag. It was okay to watch her good eye,
and the smell of hydrogen peroxide. She burned my arm
with a cigarette, and I hid it like it was a private.

We could have a religious alien experience.
Locate the new meridian, locate the burning smell.
Stand there. Glass pops, shards follow.

On the lawn, a particularly realistic doll-baby,
thick wire spiking from the end of a cable,
the feathers of two different birds. Dead thistles.

Locate the boys in the trees. They have horns
and lassos. The birds stopped giving eggs
and it's somehow our fault. Grief joins
the circle, a stranger. Streetlamps hang
their round faces over the whole scene.

When can we go home?
When a skirt is scorched,
when fists marry in long brown hair,
when the sun goes completely.

Punched holes in the empty
aluminum cans. Rolly-bugs and mud sticks
in fork tines. The long way down,
where snakes live, but no one knows a hymn.

When I came away with a bite on my back,
I was sure my spine was at risk. When I came to school
there was a pancreas and a Russian family and a movie
about monkeys that made my heart ache. I said as much.
They sent me down to speak to the lady.

At that time, they weren't so big on Greek myths.
My Leda was really disgusting. Nobody told me
what to do about it. The swan got stuck in the drain.
For a long time, I was convinced I had drowned as a baby.

That town was Dutch but the people were Republicans.
At night, we stood perilously close to the trains
and the trains were just the kind of men we'd read about.

Wanted it bad enough to go home for the day, to swallow
my tongue. Contracted one of their small plastic pirate swords.
Wanted it bad enough, doctor.

I had to read every piece of literature that mentioned them.
They carried cracked pleather purses on fool's gold chains.
They had buttery coughs, pelican wings. Maybe they were mental
and I didn't get it. These items. This waiting room.

The girl on the torn divan. Just was. Even in good dreams,
I had a wad of gum in my mouth. Woke up in one bleak sheet
with a small fish in the heart. I woke up with a hand in my dress.

My name in the mouth of a nurse. Pink soap letter from the IRS.
The table could be used, couldn't it? Open my throat, my taut
spaces, to admit fluids and pastes. Vestigial cameras finding a pearl.

There were no animals, siblings, or second stories. My visitor
wore a stiff leg like a Popsicle. B-list pajamas, hostess me!
There was an anecdote about the opposite of contagion. Me!
Wooden duck, precious little duck-duck across the bed's bar.

Finally, only the vet was willing to touch me. He took my blood out
and walked it. He took my bone out and brought me a shimmer,
without teeth marks, or an animal. Tugging and tugging.

The hysterical letter, the one-armed assassin leaning,
lurid. The slim pimp who contracts as *esquire*. For needles.
For piss-poor. The sick film, the short end, the equally slim
difference between maybe, loves me not.

The pumpkin's grin, the skeleton hand of the beautiful
rictus. The extra canine that erupts. For doctors.
For palid slices. For the shortcut through the rough alley
at a late hour. All the kids in bed.

The new thing they say when they call you.

When you started out, you had a pink dress. Each Christmas
and a ladder that led to your bed. You looked like your mother
in pictures. Your mother. She encouraged you to shave your legs.

SALTBOX BROTHEL

I was a body. I was a laboratory. I was okay with that.
We used my house, we climbed the back stairs, we told my mother
we were *meditating*. Psychic, but for her old plaid nightgown
like a cocktail dress and the glutinous straw sweating—
Her Bailey's. My looks.

On the happiest day of my life. On Presidents' Day. Upstairs,
a good citizen, my dress was big and my bed even bigger.
Three kids came. We took turns on the mattress. *Be quiet*
at regular intervals. *What next?* We used a coin.

Crossed my legs, made my pretty face, listened for my father's car.
He was a head-on. He'd be home soon. Watched a blonde head
on a brown one. Watched my own hand go down. At some point
it occurred to me, this was going to be fun.

We didn't go anywhere; we went wrong in our own backyard.
No. We didn't have a yard, but we went wrong in the bedroom.
We went wrong on uncomfortable couches, leaning against
a tiled counter. Went wrong on the linoleum.

In the winter, it was often on the stoop where it was icing, but so wrong
we didn't weather. In summer we did it when everyone else was off backpack-
ing.
When the sky and atmosphere were two different things.

We went wrong alone. I didn't mind. Mattress pads and matted hair.
I thought a lot about atoms, half-lives, projectiles, small stones in the carpet.
The asthmatic coo of pigeons sounded less and less near, but there were more
gulls, wings tapping in the long strokes of flight. Out the window.

This way of going wrong took more effort. We didn't sit up, didn't say so.
Inhaled, exhaled, watched the ceiling, fingered the shiny hem of the blanket,
took turns, took pains to turn over regularly. Took the little alarm clock to
heart.

We stopped to take a piss in a gravel lot. White at the edges,
pebbles collected. We were supposed to be there
an hour ago. Under the dashboard a small bulb, a lonely
Christmas light did its job keeping a circle in place.
I did the same, I made the *o* and components fit together.

But wasn't it a bad party? My boyfriend had his tongue
on the table, looking for something to touch it to. It wasn't ugly
between us; it was compromised. The driveway was just
another room for misgivings. The moon was punched out,
the stars had their own arguments. I made an *o*
with nothing to fill it. Someone said, *we work our way up.*
My name was everywhere; I looked around me.

We took up for each other where our families left off. Left a mess
of crumbs and beer cans. A pile of laundry. When you left town,
I kept your T-shirt in bed, synthetic residual warmth.

Used to be I'd meet you at the train tracks. My shirt too close
to my skin, my hair cramped with sexy. Used to be at night,
and red lights would come rolling across. The water below
was cut with a hacksaw.

First night in a new city, and you said it wasn't sex. She had her back
to you. When I said *I don't care,* I was in the parking lot
with my fist on my forehead. With bare feet and a bus ticket.
No ledge. No lock me in the trunk; you'd sooner lock me in the engine.

So much later you found a phone booth. Called me up
on my new red phone. I felt like the Commissioner, or like Batman
on the wrong end of things. I heard the thrum-thrum of your voice,
your lighter click, the salient signs. I took off my target T-shirt, I took off
my shiny pants. I stripped down quietly and I unplugged my lights.

Had our hands in each other's *pockets.*
When we walked the sidewalk, the cop's siren
went off like a wolf whistle, and you didn't flinch.

When you weren't around, I went at it with your boyfriend.
We never had much luck. I always wanted to go wherever
you'd gone. Once, it was Philadelphia. Dark when I got there.
Too hot to see anything but the bad paneling, stained mattress
pissing through the thin sheet.

When you were around, we took your boobs to the county fair.
There was a moment in the parking lot; we could hear the old man
selling bird whistles and plastic roses. The roses went *shhh-shhh,*
and night was a kind of big chair.

People had told us to *take it where you can get it,* and we could get it.
Lots of bottles: headless, willing. A gap in your teeth made the sound
of a stream. A hair-backed hand held out a lick of something wet.
You looked over. My shirt hung down—

It's how you do things with people you love. When my dress
was too big, you tied a string on me. A belt. You tucked
the loose end into your pants, and said *now we're related.*

RSVP

Don't invite me to your pity party.
Don't call me up on your pity party line
and invite me over for punch and cookies.
I won't come. I won't come
with a pretty pity present. I won't
put on my pity party dress with the special
ribbon in my pity pony tail. I won't play
pity pin the tail on the donkey,
or dance to pity pop music. I don't care
if the captain of the football team
and the whole pity pep squad are coming.

I don't care if your mother made her special
pineapple upside-down pity or your father plans
to grill pity pups and hamburgers. Not even
if you have an exotic pity parrot that says
Polly want some pity, or if you have the newest
model Pontiac Pity that we can drive around in.
Head up to the hills, watch the sun set
and the bright lights of the big pity turn on.

It's your party, and you know what that means,
but it's not my style. You know what I always say.
I say, *kill the people,* and *never let 'em see you sweat.*
I always say *this party's for the birds,*
and *who invited you, anyway, pal?*

CONVERSION

There was a mystery guest, like that old game "Mystery Date,"
but not as gamey. I couldn't believe the things that came
out of my mouth. Out. I had the rush rinsed out of me. Out.
I caught a scar off the burn off the heated towel rack. On the fritz.
I had the jerry-rigged baptism. Nervous. Grandma was pretty sure
it would take.

There was a mister right, a mister right now, and a mister right
around the corner. There are the kind of boxes one gets into
to tell the truth, and the other kind. A ring. A crushed glass
inside the towel. A boxing. A bar of soap in a sock.
I got the right price on a packet of geranium seeds. My pocket.
I got the token things. A little weighted hammer. Particular.

I.

I didn't appreciate the things you wore for me;
watered down T-shirts and piss-pale matchlight.
Seems it was always dusk. You pulled the cigarettes
out like a long chain of handkerchiefs. A kink in my muscle.

The grass was plain again. I was moving against it.

Proof there was nowhere to go.

My hand was the fish we should've thrown back.
A chilly *ichthus* in your lap. I admired your science.
It took the pressure off. Your hand, on the other hand,
was smart and neat. I couldn't name it; I let it go.

Go.

II.

I didn't mean to take you for granted, I meant to take you for coffee.
For a walk in the park. Each of us was a dog back then, with a leash
between our legs, in our milky white. In your bedroom, there were two
couches and loose sheets. I thought, *this is living.* You drove around
with a red door, where a door was your sleeve and your heart rusted out.
A time or two. I couldn't be your prom date. I had to pay rent.

When you showed me your tree fort, I knew it was over. Your uncle
had his pants down in the kitchen. I tried to pretend I hadn't walked in.
I tucked the pot roast into my napkin. When you hugged me goodbye,
when you felt the lump, I called it an injury and dumped it out in the bushes.

FEUD

Vertigo on the little island. Past the place that waxes a "mostash"
for five dollars, past the dollar store with Polish juice. Daddy broke
my little heart. On the outskirts of town, the outs, big fight.
I went first to his grandmother's, his wolf's house. I went next
to his island with veins. With three plywood fangs on it.
I drew myself in the sand, drew stink lines. Sticks. Drew
myself in the sea. A bath. Flat. Flat on my ass. Capital.

Rain on the island and ink on my hands. My postcards, my babies.
Past the all-night convenience with thumbprint coffee. Past
his truck in reverse, its utility steering. I went to the center,
the castle. I went through a window in the ruin headfirst,
with the extra skeleton of bad news in my body. Compression.

Coated in sentiment like old fruit in a jar, in a car whose alarm
developed a whisper, where the rope swing gave me heart attacks,
compulsion, rope burn, I couldn't be eighteen. I couldn't
marry right. Not with a crampon. Couldn't make it up the dunes;
my knees sagged. Given, as it's said, away.

III.

Now the rainman gave me two cures
then he said, "jump right in."
The one was Texas medicine
the other just railroad gin.

—BOB DYLAN

SALON

A funnel. A truly great endeavor; enclosure. Here,
a whiskey handshake in a metal glove. A turnstile
for lovers. The sardine can wears like a rosebud,
we call the cloister generous, we service the unbearable
cliquing of cliché. Dramamine.

A suitor. At the doctor's. We talked about the lovely
Herculine, as if we weren't ourselves girls about to find out
that we were actually boys finding out that we were still
a little bit girl. Infernally. We weren't ourselves the governess,
dreaming herself the renegade, tied to the tracks, untying herself
from the tracks, riding to safety, frothing as the horse does.

And the doctor conducted a series of x-rays.

A parlor game.

You can read one's fortune

by counting the blockage.

The Dutch doctor shooting my picture for a magazine ad.
He outlined my ankles with a felt marker to thin them down.
Tailbone, I liked it. We popped a really good champagne
known as widow's wine. Because it was a natural. Because
of the property tax. Because that's how long it was in the barrel.
I counted backward from reason. I counted a ventilator shaft,
venetian blinds on blackened glass, laser disk headlamp,
reference to television, practical.

In reality, science works like this: duck, duck, goose.
Like this: an empirical wild goose chase. Like:
down versus feather. Likeable little model.

MIGRAINE TRAILS A DULL NUDE

In the bath I didn't think of anything fantastic.
Not red wings on white birds. Not twinned fangs on cobras.
Not a great cat by a pearl-black river, the autumnal corpse,
the skeletal moon, or even a shadow of the sun.

None of the violet things were floating there.
None of the blue things, the iridescent things, the green things.
The water was not aspic, was not solvent, was not absinthe.
The soap was not milk soap, not scented,
not magical, or anodyne.

I did not think I heard a visitor, a thief, or ghost
beyond the bathroom door. Not a voice from heaven,
because I had not thought. I was just that pain
which sits inside the halo and cannot name anything
but its own.

DOCTOR, LET ME DO WHAT I WANT

Doctor, let me do what I want. A panic zipper
on my undercarriage. My inner carriage. Wearing proud
the vertical graveyard, each headstone, each vertebrae
ready to wear through the skin. Tensing through, a divot
of mourners, cleft spine. Each time. The orthopedist
snapped tight his glove. Mother! He found a curvature.

A Bauhaus, a peregrine.

He gave a eulogy. He wore

a pinky ring. He fit the diamond into a slot and it fit there.

Paroxysms.

SYMBIOSIS

I said something wrong in their language. I swallowed
one of their tiny coffins. A lurid rain. A telegraph
pole. I remembered clearly all the details of their stories.
Pornographic memory.

Came to my aid, came to mind. Oh, I wanted to touch
doctor's really good suit. They said *sit awhile, wait awhile.*
They had hands like a hook, line and sinker. A bird
in her well turned hole.

His suit! Dovetail, pennywhistle, RU-648. A coaster
made of litmus. A special pink tongue. All of these
were the party and the party was in my honor. A visitor.
A horse thief. I tore his sash that said *ambassador,*
I tore into his hangar.

ANESTHESIA

I swallowed one of their full-tang knives. An inflexible
incision proceeded. The stadium, to me, appeared post-
apocalyptic, but they assured me this was "normal."
The stretcher was ready. The surgeon was risen, and came
with his leather bag of liniment. A wide *w* on his sweater.

A wide-legged pyramid of supporters. My trepidation
was "unnatural." All of them agreed, it was time
to take temperature. Time to associate with a priest.
In a weak moment, the veranda seemed to come to my rescue.
Its silvery fossils. The ghost of foliage beyond the latticework.

The curly voice of a night bird. Florida. A venomous little robe.

IV.

So sweet, my Louis. What was he doing in that nest of vipers?

"I had a dream," I recall him once confiding. "It was in another century, but the doors opened and shut the same way."

—KATHRYN DAVIS

CHANTEY

Finally, I am a fishmonger's daughter. My mother,
the fishmonger's wife, brings her bucket to the light.
A blood falls out, a bulb. If the bulb cracks, I will take
the filament as a new wing, a slick, a lisp.

They sing *by the marks from the nails*. They sing *his precious
head*. Slip off the crowd. A denuding. Slip off the line.
His precious shake-shake, like a chorus girl.

The ginger lit the whiskey, the wool the wheel. Father took
his whisker out. And threaded it. Father had a place put aside
in the gutter. Where leaves went. Where skin and bones blew.

You have cancer good. You're a mean old daddy and I like you.
Too well. I consider the seat you sat in. The crown from your tooth.
I put my lips around a picket in the fence outside your bungalow.
I buy some vulgar shoes to wear to your trial. The court artist
who wants to fuck you, she took years off your pants. Off.
I stuck an emery board into the neck of every girl
who came by my office. I bound their feet. I sucked the bleach
out of their hair. Everything went like a snake. Down your pants
with my own hand. Down your pants with hers.

In my sleeper I sour. It's true, I can't pronounce the filthy thing.
My own womb. A chemical penetration from the outside.
The shower floor is slick with expensive cream. I lick you.
Your absence. My husband buries my tongue in the sand
from the lumber yard, under blue pebbles in a fish tank.
I dress for court the night before. I dress in soiled pajamas.
My rash flares.

ELECTORAL

Sat back when I knew for sure that a lot of pretty words
were just about to replace that rubber pelican. Sat back
on a tacky leather sofa and looked at those shit drapes.
That stupid Nabokov game was driving me crazy. All the letters
were coming out steel gray. All the letters were gunmetal.

On a legal pad, the Repelican next to me sketched an old woman
with menthol stink lines and the wicked names of the years
printed on her underthings. Outside it smelled like the wrong
season. Inside, too. My neighbor tugged on her lip, my neighbor
laughed politely. And really nothing was wrong with the day.

And everything was really awful. I mean really relative. I put
my hand in the purse of the woman in front of me. I pulled out
her wallet and a spray-on deodorant. I ate some dirt from a potted plant,
I licked the mailing list, I took off my shoes. But really, I was pursuing
my Ph.D. in detriment. There was nothing wrong with my pants.
There was nothing wrong with my pavilion or my maiden name,
and when they asked for my blood type, I signed away.

SICK AND TIRED

Every single time. With my hand in the cookie cutter. I mean jar.
It was the cat who gave me that cut. I came bandaged. On the council
of neighbors there was a fat neighbor who had it in for the others.
He got his car to the lot first. He got an egg salad sandwich and a plate
of paste. He called the city on me. My real name.

And a big party. I was lonely with the talk of blue breast orbiting
blue breast. I was sick with the talk of Kentucky. A horse waited.
A blue thread. A special kind of time called bourbon. A man
in a sweat suit came by with his little dog. Compunction.

Felt like a cheap crown to go with my mood.
It even looked like prom, but it was just someplace
I was living at. A girl with lukewarm hair
and a flat ass liked to come by; I went back to bed
whenever I wanted.

Could've had a ring on. Could've made my
arm an example of intent. Put my name in
the style box. Stopped pressing my luck
when it got thin enough to fit in my purse.
Everything I owned reminded me of a tampon.

Some nights I went through my own garbage.
The things people throw out. Even on good days,
the mailman made me nervous. I danced in the corner
where he couldn't see it. Not through the windows,
not with a periscope.

DURATION

It wasn't porn. It was just cards. A lot of rules. A good
cry, but not without the break-in. Wanted to fan dance
and make trouble. Instead I took a seat in the booth
and listened in. They had a good joke about Iron Maiden.
A good couple of bonnets with bees in thick glasses.

Anyhow, couldn't keep my panties on straight. Cold. Couldn't
drink the whole volcano thing so the neighbor's husband did.
Got talking. Prince, gun molls, some kind of spiced whiskey.

On the news it was all backlit. Like tiny. Whistles. Like spacemen
had come down. Those funny, American spacemen. They have
green night-vision goggles in their favor. They're not scared.
They, I mean. Sometime that evening, I stopped. Being there.

It was wrong to wear those stockings during the war. Aftershock.

A sack of same old same old. Or, how I didn't much anymore
feel like an evil twin. With Grandpa dead, no one said "a regular
Sarah Bernhardt." No one came around with his arms up. Cough,
cough. A glass of warm juice and a banana on its last legs. Eleven
pills of various sizes and aftertastes. Measure. I called the brown
horse pill. The vial of oil was *pip,* the orangey tart *momma.*

Skin like a shrug, and up to my elbows in the photo album. Picture book.
All the souvenirs were homemade. Madeleine pans. A long time gripping
the plastic dial tone, but I couldn't remember the last four digits.
To make a reservation. Make with the pony. Make with the Coca Cola
and rock candy. Nothing new or nice stayed so for long. When I wasn't
looking, the house got a hickey. Almost a suspicion, French-like.

Terrible camp stove. Terrible impersonation of dinner for one. My own hair
in the tea cup came out like a prize. The rent check was barely legible,
skulking toward morning. Hanging over. "I will tell you things" the answering
machine, the day-old paper, the bread bag with the environmental bent.
The light and the switch were almost incidental. The magnets on the cabinets.
And the only excuse for the morning news was the being up all night,
with the sound down. Flat champagne, like an antonym.

BOURG

Tried not to see the dog eating it. Tried not to smell certain trees in flower.
Harper's was weird that month. A Chinese hymen. Some sort of braised
prawns on a bed of Kant. Then strawberries came up. Small green pistols.
The birds were brave of the dog. The bird dog.

You could take an exam. A book that told clowns what to say in the class-
room.
Fu Manchu, $400 a class, the good old days. There was an essay on personal
growth. Compulsive hypergraphia. A tiny place for a plan. Everything
was really *designy*. Touching was okay. On paper.

One of those weekend encounters. Sidewalk. Bar front. Bare in the
shoulders. Your admiration meant so much to me, and I stuck my tongue
in your mouth to lick it out. That much is clear. A place for everything,
and a praise.

OR BOURG

It wasn't fair. Your husband's balls were none of my beeswax.
A blonde with so many curls we couldn't see your face. Luncheon.
The director made the female cartoonists look bad. We agreed.
But after awhile, they did look bad. Looked down. I had salad
covered with shrimp. Nouveau riche pink grapefruit. A hacksaw.

The sidewalk means Manhattan. That's just the way it is.
In the university town, my tits got bigger. Really loud.

Actually cooled off. Everyone was an urban professional;
no argument here. There were regular meetings. Toothpicks.
Refrigerator fliers. There was an awful lot of complaining,
and it sounded like lingo. Advertising jargon. We drank
compulsory champagne. Later, there was a compulsory celebration.
A dinner party. So we washed it out with bubblegum
and sent it to the navy.

THEY WERE PISS DRUNK AT THE MATINEE

They put their names on the list to leave town. In a sack of fat chances,
there may have been something to get it up for. In movies,
small towns are the source of love, witches, and premarital sex.
A towel shoved under the door. Matchsticks and Vapo-Rub.
Some kind of plain metal can.

Their favorite song said my heart is a rocket. My heart has a loose hinge.
A ray gun and a helmet. My heart got tanked on Jim B. and sod-y-pop.
They put their names on the list to leave town. Waited. Opened
the mailbox with a razorblade and some pepper spray. A tourniquet.
The mailbox was always half drunk.

The last thing they said as they left the party was swept up in the cold
porch wind. The swing made a noise like a man on a date and the man
on the date spun his date on her heels. Red heels halfway down the sidewalk.
They held a match to the key, she to an eyeliner, he under his palm,
and she to the end of a fishing line. They put a rock in the pillowcase.

Even in good dreams, I couldn't get my top off.
It rained for three days straight, and everything
collected a cold skin. The refrigerator
made a noise like a bird, the birds made a noise
like a washer, and water soaked in near the chimney.

On the weekend, the flea market was more of
a ghost town, and the junk shops were just that.
I couldn't find tiles, I couldn't find telescopes.
I guess I thought I was closer to home;
I called to ask if it was raining, but everyone laughed,
and then they said *don't worry about the downsize.*

A list. Take shopping. Take care. Take singing off-key.
Alone at the table. What a mess. What a fly new haircut.
What a surprise; the horse-look never struck me sexy.
And then it stopped restructuring. We got some sunlight,
these industrious woodpeckers. On a dead limb, a dog's tooth.

It was a long ten days. When the mail came, the man came
and gave me the eye. Honestly, his eyes were everywhere.
Thing. Couldn't have made it go faster. Instead, I took tons.
Sudafed, or generic from Israel. 1996. As though a frothy,
solitary cookie. Even in good dreams I had one in the bag.
The back burner, maybe.

Got time delay on the phone line. Got an eviction notice.
Or the other way around. Anyhow, the newsprint smelled
like an old car. Cassettes on the floor, empty shells, a rag,
a bottle of something. Bedded. Super.

Got the little bit of heartbreak. Got the cracked goods
packed up in the box. Liquor store. Package store.
Whether or not the men got the dead limb, they got limbs
by the dozen. A tourniquet for a tree. A caftan or wrapper.

The inside of the child's arm looked like the fancy lining of a dull cape.
She raised it like a wing, sure. Raised by wolves. By lamb limbs
with sharp buds. She pointed out Tyrannosaurus Rex,
Mark Twain, and Sir Lancelot.

The truck came with all its wheels mincing. A couple of piss-pants
got in the way with a petition. A dogwood. The landlord
pocketed his keys like his pants were padlocked. The picnic
was canceled. The picnic was no good. The neighbors got loaded.

And so did the truck. It was April. It was good to go.
Whether or not the tree made it, the roof looked less suspicious.
They were almost sorry. They were out in a heartbeat. A flash.
No, a heartbeat.

That house was full of furniture I'd never been tied to. I saw
a lamp and called it a halo. A small deformity. A hook in the frame
went off at an angle. My towel dropped away in the doorway.
I gave you a time capsule full of lead paint. To bury a babyhood.
I gave you the pelvic bone of a six-year-old girl. A dollar.

Where was the teapot the cat broke, the brooch, the figurine?
When your grandmother called you to her bed, you went, and I.
And I was on the patio. The lawn. The neighbor's lawn.

The phone showed its sick root to me last night. It wanted
to call you. A tremor, a wound worm in the pillowcase.

PASTORAL

Moonflowers edging the corn stand, singing the hallelujah portion
of "It's Raining Men" over and over. In a whinny. Trouble to keep
all those little hands and feet inside the vehicle. In East Hangover.
With white eggplant. With aubergine eggplant. Moonshine, sugar,
mint and grit in the bottom of a teacup.

Not to stick an elbow in an ear or a love note in the glove
compartment. Talking away from the covered bridge. Talking.
It was raining men. It was raining small hearts cut from construction
paper. Embalmed. It was a raining. A times. A wailing.
The sweetheart, thief, in a Batesian mask. A corncob pipe bomb.

At the end of *Oklahoma,* only the haystack was burning. The surrey.

ACKNOWLEDGMENTS

Poems from *Pretty Young Thing* have appeared in the anthologies *The Best American Poetry 2004* (Scribner 2004) and *Bend, Don't Shatter* (Soft Skull 2004), and in *Black Warrior Review, canwehaveouballback?*, the *Canary, Carolina Quarterly, Columbia Poetry Review, Conduit, Crowd, eye-rhyme, Good Foot, La Petite Zine, LIT, Lungfull!, Painted Bride Quarterly, Pleiades, Poetry Daily, Skein*, the *tiny*, and *Unpleasant Event Schedule*.

The quotation on page 7 is from *Dialogues in Paradise* by Can Xue, translated by Ronald R. Janssen and Jian Zhang, Northwestern University Press, 1989.

The quotation on page 25 is from "Suppôts et supplications" by Antonin Artaud, as quoted by Julia Kristeva's *Powers of Horror*, translated by Leon S. Roudiez, Columbia University Press, 1982.

The poem "RSVP" on page 41 borrows the phrase "kill the people" from the film *All About Eve*.

The quotation on page 47 is from "Stuck Inside of Mobile with those Memphis Blues Again" by Bob Dylan.

The poem "Migraine Trails a Dull Nude" on page 51 takes its form from Wallace Stevens's "Disillusionment at Ten O'Clock."

On page 53, RU-648 is not RU-486.

The quotation on page 55 is from *Versailles* by Kathryn Davis, Houghton Mifflin, 2002.

The poem on page 58 borrows the line "You're a mean old daddy, but I like you," from "Carey" by Joni Mitchell.

"They Were Piss Drunk at the Matinee" on page 67 refers to Geoff Reacher's song "The Freak," which includes the phrase "my heart is a rocket."

THANK YOU

Most grateful thanks to the following: Everyone at Soft Skull Press, and in particular, Richard Nash, Shanna Compton (an extraordinary editor!), Daniel Nester, and David Janik. Christa Parravani, photographer and Jed Berry, a willing model. David Lehman, Susan Wheeler, and Joyelle McSweeney for their thoughtful, highly valued readings and commentary. All my workshop and seminar teachers past and present, and the many classmates who have given their time and consideration to this manuscript in its various incarnations. Lara Glenum, Johannes Goransson, Kirsten Kaschock, Sabrina Orah Mark, Jeffrey Salane, Heidi Lynn Staples, and Adrienne Vrettos for their patience, advice, and/or support. Those editors who included poems from this book in their fine publications. Above all, Adam Henne, Hazel Henne, and dog Clea.

ABOUT THE AUTHOR

Danielle Pafunda was born in Albany, New York. She received her BA from Bard College and MFA from New School University. She is currently pursuing her PhD with Creative Dissertation at the University of Georgia, where she teaches creative writing and English composition, and is an editorial assistant for the *Georgia Review*. *Pretty Young Thing* is her first collection. Her second manuscript *My Zorba* was a recent finalist for the University of Massachusetts Press's Juniper Prize for Poetry, and Four Way Books's Levis Poetry Prize. She has appeared in *The Best American Poetry 2004*, and been nominated for Pushcart Prizes and the anthology *Best New Poets 2005*. She is coeditor of the online journal *La Petite Zine* and lives in Athens, Georgia.